Letters, Unwritten

Andrew Robin

Winner of the Two Sylvias Press Chapbook Prize

Copyright © 2024 Andrew Robin

All rights reserved. No part of this book may be reproduced in any form without the written permission of the publisher, except for brief quotations embodied in critical articles and reviews.

Two Sylvias Press
PO Box 1524
Kingston, WA 98346
twosylviaspress@gmail.com

Cover Design: Kelli Russell Agodon
Book Design: Annette Spaulding-Convy
Contest Judge: Eduardo C. Corral

Created with the belief that great writing is good for the world, Two Sylvias Press mixes modern technology, classic style, and literary intellect with an eco-friendly heart. We draw our inspiration from the poetic literary talent of Sylvia Plath and the editorial business sense of Sylvia Beach. We are an independent press dedicated to publishing the exceptional voices of writers.

For more information about Two Sylvias Press please visit:
www.twosylviaspress.com

First Edition. Created in the United States of America.

ISBN: 978-1-948767-22-4

Two Sylvias Press

Praise for *Letters, Unwritten*

These short epistolary poems are dazzling, rich with surprising language. (To be honest, I wish I'd written some of these lines.) Here, surprise is a prism; it refracts loneliness, grief, humor, and forgiveness. The recipient of these letters is unknown—it doesn't matter. What matters more is the linguistic pleasures leaping off each page, the way language not addressed to us can sometimes resonate like intimacy.

—**Eduardo C. Corral**, Contest Judge

You, gone.
Without desiring the word
I had in my heart and didn't know how to say.

~ Antonia Pozzi

Dear X,

I dragged your piano into the snow.
Through my own breaths, beyond sleeping people.

The black trees shouldered in.
My gasoline and I, we were beautiful in no moonlight.

Now, a match-head cracked like a wronged
and ravenous seed. Now the ancient

ebon grain, the glazed flesh flaking
off in strips. O the willing

smoke. The ruined orb
of the sky.

Dear X,

I look out at the slick
and naked winter trees

thrust up like lungs to the skyful
body of day. They are older

than anything I know. The sparrows
touch them tenderly, like one might

a grandmother beloved and forgetful
and inching toward the dominion of god.

Is this the song these beasts
can't help but sing?

That stirs in them such
deep and reverent

trust in loss?

Dear X,

I have taken a machete to your paper wolves.

They put up no fight. Simply folded into
themselves and offered silence for howls.

As if love and cold time were sucking
their beauty back into the earth.

I'm sorry.

I am sorry they were not
the wolves I needed

them to be.

Dear X,

The sky is following me.

As if I carry something borrowed it wants back.
Three dollars. A bad heart. —What?

Sticks of warm gum.

The patient, waiting bird
of the soul.

Dear X,

How much loneliness must we inherit?

For instance: a child with an asterisk
nailed in place of a heart.

But who nailed it there?
It was snowing, it was difficult to see.

There was an explosion of crows.
An orchestra of darkness commenced:

It could have been anyone.

It was a season of
many orphans.

Dear X,

I trapped old winter in one piano note.

The crows came down from the limbs to see.
And commenced fighting over it.

I let them fight.

Snow flew up, shards of noise.
Should is a paralyzing word.

Perhaps to be a witness

of beauty is
enough.

Dear X,

I am befriended by a tree.

Asleep in that gnarled bosom,
I dream the crocuses out from their graves.

A swallowtail summits me.
The grass is here. Shifts of wind.

The heartwood thrums.
It's spring.

I'm no
one.

Dear X,

Your bison:

with their gleaming
perfect eyes, lumbering to me

across the expanse, sniffing as if
I had come for them with food or love.

Your bison: so diminutive in the distance
and still tiny here in the flesh: so perfect one

might scoop them into a palm, stroke their
downy throats. The glinting horns,

the imaginary names—I slipped them
in a pocket. I carry them everywhere.

A warm and writhing gift. But
who is it for? This secret, this

fabulous prize I haven't
the liberty or virtue

to give.

Dear X,

I have done
what I was warned

against and filled my
inexorable emptiness with cats.

Omnipresent, they prowl the house
and grounds. They inspect, and kill, and

sleep, curled, sprawled, everywhere.
Yes, a facet of my aloneness is

assuaged. A blessing for which
I have paid dearly in

birdsong.

Dear X,

I step to the edge of the page.

The darkness out there is swimming with owls.
And has each of them swallowed a star?

They are bright in the belly like agates.

They are circling back,
now they dip through me,

through my shadow as if we are ink.

I lie down in the center as in unmarked snow.
I am part of this now. Here they come,

winging over the drifts,
bringing my poem.

Dear X,

Followed all day through the storm by the soul of a wolf.

And why not? In my life I have stolen from
and lied to everyone I love. I've said

irreconcilable things. Perhaps she is hungry.
Or lonely. Perhaps she carries in her maw

the bone of forgiveness for me?
My rough tracks in the drifts:

the storm opening, closing
unmoved around me,

like endless sky
around a

bird.

Dear X,

Pears,

as if floating,
daubed like goldleaf

against a heavy snow. And deer,
come red and chestdeep through the drifts

to sniff and bare their soft white throats.
(Who painted this kept a pack of docile

wolves in the evenings of their heart.)
Hoofprints, startled, and then

launched into flawless
leaps over the earth.

Pears: faintly swinging,

with little crescent
moons bitten

out.

Dear X,

And here is old scarecrow,

dangling unnamed on his stick in the rain.
Abandoned, stuffed with dead news, one eye

plucked out. He's scanning the treeline
for enemy shapes, devoted still

to those who abandoned
him here. He reminds me

of me before I thought
I was worthy of love

in this world.

Dear X,

Today a person spoke to me.

It was a concierge of the Queen Nefertari exhibit,
who said, Go on past the cat-faced goddess

Sekhmet, and down the red carpeted stairs.
You will pass Anubis' crypt and a severed-

head statue. Beyond that a tiger is
clutching an ibex in its fangs.

Beyond that is a falcon with
amethyst eyes. The restroom

is just there. Enjoy
your visit.

Dear X,

Sometimes I know
what to make of the world.

Sometimes I just walk
amongst people,

touching my
shadow to

theirs.

Dear X,

I watch a child

on the Tillikum Ferry passenger deck
hoist aloft a cold french fry,

lift it into a single beam of sun:

At once she is haloed in gulls
who jostle, mewling,

to touch her hair,
to be near her beauty,

who gleam
and sing,

almost
holy.

Dear X,

Each time your name
happens to fall from a passing

bird's shadow and tumble into the iced grasses,
silence becomes me. And I am lifted briefly over

my life like a christ of snowlight. Beaming,
and then set down to earth, where I am

no one again. Though for many
days after, I taste lightning.

I hear stars.

Dear X,

I'm sorry
I could not keep

my appointment with that cloud.

We abandon ourselves,
do you understand

this?

Dear X,

I trudged out to visit your piano's bones.

Glazed in ice, they arced
and gleamed like animals

paused in their becoming.

Gorgeous, sweeping nothings.

No bird awake, no shift of light:
the silence closing in on itself.

A white and final room.

I would tell you I knelt down
and prayed. I would tell you

I lay back in the fallout
like some angel and

forgave the
world.

Acknowledgements

*Bear Review, Bennington Review,
The Main Street Rag, Molecule, Timberline Review.*

Andrew Robin lives with his wife Sarah on Sx'wálech (Lopez Island) in the unceded ancestral waterways of the Coast Salish peoples, where he works as a registered nurse. He is the author of *something has to happen next* from University of Iowa Press, *good beast* from Burnside Review Books, and *Stray Birds* from Kelson Books. His work is anthologized in *An Introduction to the Prose Poem* and *Field Guide to Prose Poetry*. Andrew is the recipient of a distinguished teaching award in English from the University of Massachusetts Amherst.

www.ingramcontent.com/pod-product-compliance
Lightning Source LLC
Chambersburg PA
CBHW051706040426
42446CB00009B/1330